MARTIN WILLIAMS AND DR. JIM CAIN

101 Games To Play While Physically Distancing

For All Ages

Copyright © 2021 by Martin Williams and Dr. Jim Cain

All rights reserved. No part of this publication may be reproduced, stored or transmitted in any form or by any means, electronic, mechanical, photocopying, recording, scanning, or otherwise without written permission from the publisher. It is illegal to copy this book, post it to a website, or distribute it by any other means without permission.

First edition

*This book was professionally typeset on Reedsy.
Find out more at reedsy.com*

Contents

1	Your Free Book	1
2	Introduction	3
3	Circle Games	8
4	Ice-Breakers	17
5	Relay Races	24
6	The Dutchman's Rope	31
7	Partner Games	42
8	Mindfulness Circle Games	47
9	Classic Game Variations	52
10	Active Physical Distancing Games	57
11	I'm In Games	66
12	Challenge Games	71
13	Fun Zoom Games Across The Curriculum	79
14	Active Virtual Games	87
15	101 Additional Physically Distanced Activities	94
16	Risk Assessment Checklist	105
17	Best Practices To Minimize Risk	107
18	What The Research Tells Us	110
19	References And Resources	112
20	About The Authors	115
Also by Martin Williams and Dr. Jim Cain		120

1

Your Free Book

Your Free Book Is Waiting

How do you get children excited about numbers when playing outside? How can you inspire outstanding progress in mathematics through outdoor learning? How can you set up engaging activities on a limited budget?

This beautifully illustrated book provides 50 inspirational number activities for children aged 3 to 6.

Download '50 Outdoor Number Activities On A Budget' Free At This Link Below

https://earlyimpactbooks.com/50-games/

101 GAMES TO PLAY WHILE PHYSICALLY DISTANCING

Download for free at - *https://earlyimpactbooks.com/50-games/*

2

Introduction

To chart our current way forward as educators and facilitators, we need to really understand what children have been through in the pandemic.

They have experienced separation and isolation like never before.

They have lived exclusively indoors, and many have experienced hopelessness, lack of human connection, and lack of real-life interaction in unprecedented quantities.

Parts of life that had been so simple and crucial before were suddenly no longer allowed. Giving someone a hug became a matter of life-or-death. So simple an action, that has been shown to have so many positive psychological benefits, has simply been banned, and may well be for the foreseeable future.

Martin Williams and Jim Cain teamed up on this book to share their experience in teaching and inspiring teachers, educators and camp leaders around the world.

Before looking at the solutions, we first looked at the problems...

Lack Of Connection

Commonplace things like shaking hands have literally been replaced by nothing.

What else has bitten the dust? Sitting next to your friends, hugging, sharing equipment, holding hands…and so many more things.

Research has shown the terrible consequences this lack of human contact can have on children. But how can we re-introduce connection to other people while maintaining appropriate physical distancing?

Indoor Living

Over the last year, many children have experienced a larger 'nature-deficit' than ever before.

What does this look like? Nature calms children down, helps their cognitive functions, and also boosts their immune system and physical health. These are benefits that many children will have been without over a long period.

Mental Health

Much of the research data associated with prolonged periods of isolation have to do with three specific populations: orphans, test animals and astronauts.

To study such research in detail is, so to speak, not a pretty endeavor. And yet, the results of these studies have yielded some profound details that can be applied to our present situation – the long-term psychological effects of a global pandemic.

These issues for some will be deep rooted. Some children will have experienced traumas, attachment problems, bereavement, and many other psychological issues. The full impact of these experiences will be felt over the years to come.

Sedentary Lifestyle

This whole generation of children has moved less in the last year than any generation before it.

Moving is a child's natural state of being. They are made to move, and we have fully embraced this concept throughout this book.

The Solutions (Or At Least Part Of It)

While there may be no absolute 'solution' to life after a global pandemic, we believe the activities and best practices presented in this book will address many of the most prominent concerns created in the past year.

We shared literally hundreds of ideas together, and in the end have come up with the ultimate selection of 101 activities that can be played in the context of physical distancing.

Unlike the first two books in this series, these are games that can be played for all ages. This is the major difference between this book and it's two predecessors.

These games target the key issues we face. We want to get children outside, interacting together, moving, and feeling a part of a group.

The activities encourage teamwork, but done so in a physically distanced way. They develop human connection, but again done safely. They encourage mindulness, well-being, cooperation, enjoyment, physical activity, and fun.

The activities are split into some of the most popular key themes: ice-breakers, circle games, active activities, classic games, mindfulness activities, partners games, relay races. Basically there are learning experiences across the entire curriculum.

All can be played outdoors, and we recommend doing that as much as is possible. However, the majority could definitely be played indoors if required.

Objects and props are kept to an absolute minimum in the games. More than half require no equipment at all. The others have simple resources that are handled by just one person throughout the game.

There has been a huge demand for online learning over the past year, and so we have included two dozen games that can be presented in virtual space.

All of the online learning games are based around the same principles as the rest of the book - they are fun and interactive, with an emphasis on building connection. The online learning games are all fantastic to use as brain-breaks, or for throwing into other virtual learning lessons and sessions.

If 101 activities isn't enough for you, we've also included a bonus chapter of 101 more ideas that can all be done within the context of physical distancing.

We have also included guidance on best practice. There is a checklist on how to minimize risk in any activity, and guidance on how to risk assess and understand current safety policies.

INTRODUCTION

All in all, we hope we have provided a resource that can be your go-to guide at this time. All the activities can be used by teachers, professionals, camp leaders, and anyone else that works with children of any age. If you're looking for physically distanced games for all ages, then everything you require can be found in the following pages.

Good luck bringing joy, connection, and interaction to children's lives through your use of the ideas in this book, and best wishes as we rebuild and reconnect in the new normal and beyond.

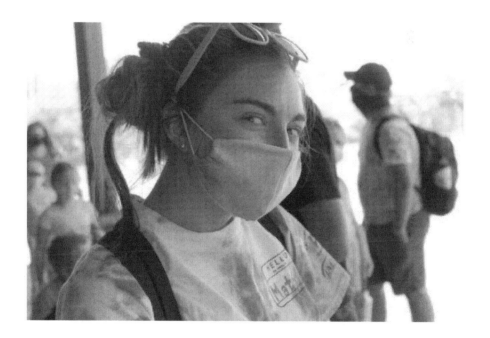

3

Circle Games

Circle games could have been made for physical distancing.

They keep participants apart as a natural feature of their rules, but they do this in a way that is fun and not over-bearing.

Also, circle games are often all about social skills - eye-contact, trust, teamwork, cooperation, and all the other things that children need to counterbalance the isolation of physical distancing.

These circle games could all be played with something like rubber spots on the ground to mark positions in a wide circle. Alternatively, you could just ask the players to spread out.

CIRCLE GAMES

1. Eyes Shut Count

The eyes open version of this game is easy. But this is the hard version – with eyes shut!

The players sit in a circle, and close their eyes. Nominate one person to start, and they are going to say, 'One'. The person next to them is going to say, 'Two.' And so on like that around the circle.

Sounds simple! But children often find this game hilarious. They are all on edge, listening out for the person next to them to speak. It is great for recognizing the voices of your friends, and there are usually lots of funny mistakes.

If you really want to ratchet up the difficulty, you could do something like counting backwards, or counting in multiples of a number.

2. Eyes Shut Beep Count

This is a more complex version of the game above.

When the players are counting this time, they only count from 1 to 10. When you get to 10 each time, you go back to one.

However – here's the twist – the second time you count, the player that says '10' will also suggest a number that next time is going to be 'beep'. They might say, '10…and 4.' That means that the team will not say the number '4' next time – they will only say 'beep.' For that round of counting it would sound a bit like, '1, 2, 3, beep, 5…' etc.

Count to ten again (with the 'beep' added), and then the next person to say ten suggests another number that will be 'beep'. This is added to the first, i.e. '4' in the example.

So, if it was '7', the next round of counting would go, '1…2…3…beep…5…6…beep….8…'

All this takes place with your eyes closed as well, so very tricky!

3. Speed Treasure Hunt

Everyone sits in a circle for this one, apart from one volunteer that is going to stand in the middle with their eyes shut.

One object is silently put on the ground at some point in the circle.

When someone says, 'Go,' the person in the middle is going to try to find the object as fast as possible and pick it up. The players in the circle are going to try to help the person find the object.

You could do different alternative rules for this, including:
   -Try against the clock
   -Half the players are helping, the others are trying to trick the person in the middle!

4. Pirate's Treasure

This communication activity requires two teams of four people.

Team One has a blindfolded 'seeker' that is on their hands and knees trying to find an object in the grass. There are also two 'lookers' who can see the 'seeker' but cannot speak, and one 'communicator' that can speak and who can see the 'lookers' but has their back to the 'seeker' so they cannot see them.

Team One has a blindfolded 'whomper' who wields a long foam pool noodle and tries to contact (whomp!) the 'seeker'. There are also two 'lookers' and one 'communicator' in Team Two.

Each team is trying to be the first to complete their task. The 'seeker' is trying to find an object in the grass, such as a tennis ball, stuffed animal or even a cowbell. The 'whomper' is trying to contact the 'seeker' with their foam noodle.

The 'lookers' are giving hand motion instructions to the 'communicator' who is shouting directions to the 'seeker' (or 'whomper').

First team to accomplish their task twice, wins! Then have team members change roles and play again.

5. Missing Player Game

This game can starts easily enough, but can become more challenging if desired.

One person volunteers to be 'on'. They go away from the circle of players, so that they definitely cannot see them.

In the simplest version of the game, one player from the circle will then go away and hide somewhere where they can't be seen. It might be behind a door or a tree.

The person that is 'on' comes back, and tries to guess who is missing.

You can make this much harder by adding more players. There could be three or four people that vanish.

6. Swap Places Vanish

This is a combination of two ideas, and can be played in different ways.

It is based on the previous 'Missing Player Game'.

This time, when the person who is 'on' goes off and closes their eyes, one person will go away and hide from the circle, and also the others will all swap places. This makes it much trickier when the person comes back to work out who is missing.

The super-hard version is when five or six people leave the circle, and everyone swaps places as well. Good luck with that!

7. One Lion, Rah!

This is a circle game that gets progressively harder as you keep on going.

The children sit in a physically distanced circle for this. The first person in the circle says, 'One lion.'

Then the next person says, 'Two eyes.' The next person says, 'Four legs.' And the next player goes, 'Rah!'

The sequence continues like this: the next person in the circle now says, 'Two lions.' Then, 'Four eyes.' Next person says, 'Eight legs!' And the next player says, 'Rah! Rah!'

Keep going like this. Next it would be, 'Three lions...six eyes...twelve legs... Rah! Rah! Rah!'

8. Pass That Noise

This is another game that is incredibly easy with eyes open, but much more challenging with eyes closed - and that's the way we suggest that you play it!

Players sit in a physically distanced circle. One person is going to be the 'leader' and will create the noises first. It would make sense for this to be either an adult or a child that has played before and is confident to create noises.

The first person is going to make some kind of noise towards the person sitting next to them. Although they have their eyes closed, they are going to 'pass' that noise to the next person, and they will pass it on, and so on around the circle.

Some good noises to try include:
 -Farm animals
 -Jungle animals
 -Character voices, like a ghost going 'woo!', or a cackling witch
 -Sound effects, like fireworks going 'ffff', or something going 'bang!'

9. Count Clap

This is a circle game, with counting as the main focus.

In this game, you first pick one number that the children are not allowed to say. As well as not being able to say the number, they also cannot say any multiples of it either, or a number that features that numeral in it. For example, you might say the number is 'five'. Therefore the children are not allowed to say the number 5, any multiples of 5 (such as 10, 15, 20 etc), and also any numbers with a 5 in it (like 53, 59, and anything else like that).

When the number comes up, instead they have to clap.

The lower the number, the harder the game! If the number is 'two', for example, this means that all even numbers are basically out, as well as all the twenties.

10. Dance Your Name

Who can resist a little name-based boogie!

This is an ice-breaker, mixed with a literacy activity, combined with a circle game - so there's lots of skills going on.

One child stands up, and they are going to present their name in the form of dance. The idea is to break your name up into its syllables, with associated dance moves.

So 'Ste-pha-nie' might do a great dance routine of three moves, such as, 'twist to the left' (Ste-), 'twist to the right' (pha-), 'jump in the air' (nie!).

Everyone copies the routine (and you could try it a few times). Then the person next to them has a go of leading the name-dance.

11. Circle Race

Here's a circle game combined with a race.

The children sit in a physically distanced circle. Go round the circle, giving everyone a number from 1 to 4. So you go a bit like, '1, 2, 3, 4, 1, 2, 3, 4...etc'

Then call out a number, for example, '4!'

All the '4s' are going to jump up, and then it's a race. They are going to do one lap around the outside of the circle, before getting back to their original place and sitting down. The first one back is the champion.

When all the numbers have had a go, you could have one last 'champion of champions' race to finish off.

12. Seven

Standing in an appropriately distanced circles of about six players, one player counts aloud, ONE.

The next player counts, TWO.

THREE, FOUR, FIVE, SIX... but instead of saying SEVEN, the seventh person CLAPS (which counts as the SEVEN and REVERSES the direction of the count).

The next person says EIGHT, and the count continues in this direction until they reach FOURTEEN, at which point they switch directions again, until SEVENTEEN, when again the direction changes.

So, if there is a SEVEN, a multiple of SEVEN, such as TWENTY-ONE or the number has a seven in it, such as SEVENTEEN, that person CLAPS instead of saying the number. The goal is for the group to get to FIFTY without making a mistake.

Groups typically struggle near the TWENTY-SEVEN / TWENTY-EIGHT mark, but eventually they all get to FIFTY. If your group is really capable, you can also try counting from FIFTY-ONE to ONE HUNDRED, but things get a bit tricky when they reach SEVENTY!

4

Ice-Breakers

We can all still become acquainted with others within the context of physical distancing. The following games are all team-builders that help children interact, loosen up, and understand those around them better.

1. Imaginary Ball

For this game, stand in a physically distanced circle. No props are required.

Players start to pass round an imaginary ball. They literally do the passing movement, one at a time to each other.

After a couple of revolutions of the circle, mix things up by introducing different ways of passing the ball. For example, they can kick it to the person next to them. Or they could bounce it.

Get more and more imaginative as the game goes on, and see what they can come up with - using knees, elbows, heading, using the back of the foot - whatever they can think of to propel that imaginary ball!

As a second variation, instead of throwing an imaginary ball, toss another interesting object such as a cement block, bowling ball, tennis racket, a small elephant, or whatever else they can think of.

2. Fly!

One leader is required for this, either an adult or a child that knows how to play the game well.

Everyone stands in a space over a wide area.

The leader gives instructions, based on different animals that are flying. For example, they might say, 'Horses fly!' If the animal in question does not fly in reality, then the players freeze on the spot.

On the other hand, the leader might say an animal that really does fly, such as, 'Geese fly!' When this happens, everyone starts flapping their wings, and flying round the space like geese.

With the next instruction, either carry on flying (if it is a flying animal), or freeze (if it doesn't fly).

The players can fly in different styles based on whatever animals it is. Eagles could soar, or humming birds could flap their wings really fast.

3. Change Three Things

This activity begins by inviting partners to carefully study each other's appearance, gathering as much detail as possible.

Then, once each person has a vivid picture of their partner's appearance, these two partners turn back-to-back.

Next, each person changes three things about their appearance. For example, they might roll their sleeves up, change the position of a clip in their hair, have one pocket hanging out, or whatever else they can think of.

When both partners are ready, they turn around and see if they can identify what is now different about their partner, all while maintaining appropriate physical distancing.

4. Walking And Talking

In this get-acquainted activity, partners take a stroll together. As they walk, they attempt to find three unusual and incredibly interesting commonalities that they share. The more unique the connection, the better.

Once these partners have found three commonalities, invite them to share these connections with another group of two.

To maintain appropriate physical distancing during this activity, you can give each pair a foam pool noodle to hold between them, or walk along a paved walkway, using the sidewalk as the separation distance, or create a physically distanced path on your athletic court using masking tape or sidewalk chalk.

5. Long-Distance Greetings

Unfortunately, handshakes are a no-go with physical distancing.

However, there are still lots of imaginative non-contact handshakes you can attempt. These are great for imagination, team-building and cooperation.

One way of playing this game is to have two lines of physically distanced rubber spots or cones on the ground, the two lines being about three yards apart. Have the same number of markers as you have kids in the game.

Players run to a vacant marker, and face a partner. They try some kind of non-contact handshake. Once completed, they change positions, finding a new maker and a new partner to try the next handshake on.

You can try the more structured version of the game first, by demonstrating

ICE-BREAKERS

some of the following handshakes, and getting the players to try them out with the partner that they are facing:

The Wave – Raise your dominant hand over your head and wave while saying loudly "Yoo-hoo!"

The Salute – In rigid military style, salute your partner.

Fist to Palm & Bow – In the style of martial arts, make a fist with your dominant hand and place it in the open palm of your other hand, then bow.

Tip of the Hat – A throwback to earlier times. Reach up with your dominant hand, holding the brim of your imaginary hat. Lift it, tip it, and place it back on your head, all while maintaining eye contact with your partner.

Standing Ovation – Raise both hands above your head, making a giant letter O, then applaud your partner while clapping loudly.

The Soccer Player – Use both knees to keep an imaginary soccer ball aloft, then drop it to the ground and kick it to your partner.

The Baseball Player – Version I – One partner takes on the role of a baseball pitcher, winding up and throwing an imaginary fast ball at their partner, who swings like a batter. Version II – One partner tosses an imaginary baseball into the air, then hits it with an imaginary bat as their outfield partner prepares to catch it.

Two Jugglers – In this final version of creative non-contact greetings, partners attempt to juggle several imaginary tennis balls, passing them back and forth between each other.

When everyone is acquainted with these different 'handshakes', you can try a free-flow version of the game, where they just run to a different marker and attempt whatever idea they like. You can also allow time for the partners to invent their own 'handshakes' and demonstrate them to the group.

In addition to these creative long-distance greetings, you can also turn this activity into a name game by asking partners to share their names with each other as they perform their greetings.

6. Wrapped Around My Finger

For this popular icebreaking activity, each person involved needs to first remove one lace from their shoe. You could also supply a piece of string or yarn for each person to use and then discard.

'Wrapped Around My Finger' is an opportunity for each member of the group to introduce themselves as they slowly wrap a shoelace around their finger. Some people refer to this process as Wrapping & Rapping.

The physical act of wrapping the shoelace around their index finger occupies the part of the brain that controls nervousness, making it easier for individuals to introduce themselves to a new group, and the length of the shoelace or string invites individuals to share more than just their name and where they are from.

The longer the shoelace or string, the greater the amount of information shared.

7. My Lifeline

To prepare for this icebreaking activity you'll need to find or create several long lines on the floor or ground.

These could be the lines on a basketball or volleyball court, the lines of a parking lot, lines drawn with chalk on a sidewalk or lines created with rope or string. Each line should be at least ten feet long. These lines represent the entire lifetime of one individual, from beginning to end.

Then form physically distanced groups of three and invite one of these three people to share some of the major milestones of their life. There obviously isn't time to share everything that has happened, so just five or six of the major life events will suffice.

When finished, another member of the trio begins to walk the line, sharing several of their major life events. Continue the activity until every member of each trio has had the opportunity to share.

8. The Walk of Life

This is another game where the players are in trios.

One person goes first. They take ten steps and mention one significant milestone in their lives for each step.

The other two participants follow the speaker on their journey. Then another member of the trio would strike off in a new direction, sharing ten significant life events, followed by the third and final member of the group.

Depending on the time and space available, you can alter the number of milestones for each speaker. Maintain physical distancing for this event by inviting participants to raise their arms (like airplane wings) and flying in formation for each of the three speakers.

5

Relay Races

Here are a selection of relay races that keep children apart, but get them moving and interacting in all sorts of fun ways.

Get the children to sit in some kind of physically distanced way, and you are good to go.

There is no tagging or passing of batons in any of these races. It is more the case that when one player has had their go, and they sit back down in their original space, then the next person goes.

1. Shoe Race

In this relay, all players take off their shoes, and place them all about 50 yards away from where their team is sitting. They place them in pairs, in a physically distanced line. It's important that the shoes for each team are equally distant from where they are sitting (to make the race fair).

Players sit in physically distanced lines.

The idea of this race is that the first player in each team runs to their team's shoes, picks out one of their own shoes, and runs back to their team. They sit and put their one shoe on as the next person goes.

Each person in turn runs and collects one shoe, before bringing it back and putting it on.

When everyone has gone, the first person goes again, now running with one shoe on. They collect their second shoe and bring it back. Then the next person goes.

The winning team are those that are the first to be sitting in a line with their shoes on!

2. Who Am I Relay

No props are required for this race at all, which is always a bonus.

The teams sit in physically distanced lines, and one player from each team goes to sit about fifty yards in front of their team. They sit with their backs to their teammates.

'Ready, set, go!' The first player in each team will run towards where their teammate is in the distance, and stop just behind them. They say, 'Who am I?'

The person with their back turned has got to guess who the player is. As soon as they guess correctly, the player is able to run back to their team, and the next player goes. (They can have a few guesses if required).

This is a voice recognition game.

Another way of playing is when the person who guesses has got the name right, the two players swap positions. The runner becomes the sitter, and the person that was sitting runs back to join the team.

3. Silly Moves Cards

For this race, you need one set of cards for each team. The cards will have pictures of the types of moves that the players could do.

For example, you might have a set of animal cards. It could have pictures of a 'horse', a 'monkey', a 'snake', and a 'tiger.'

One person in each team is in control of the cards, and only they touch them. They show a card to the first person in the team. That person will run to a designated point and back, but moving in the way it states on the card. So, if it is the 'snake' card, they will be slithering on their bellies!

Some moves are much trickier and more time-consuming than others, so a team may sometimes have a big lead in the race, but it can be one that could be wiped away in no time.

4. Zombie Run Zombie

Have some kind of loud instrument, or even an airhorn for this race. The only other props that are required are some kind of cones, one for each team.

The players start in a physically distanced line. Place one cone directly in front of each team, about fifty yards in front of them (or shorter if you prefer).

The first players in each team will be running to the cone and back. However, the trick is that whenever you hear the instrument (or airhorn), you have to transform into a zombie!

Players will then be running with straight legs, and their arms straight out in front of them. Whenever they sit down, the next player goes (no tagging in these relay races). If the airhorn or instrument has not sounded again, then the second player will also be moving like a zombie.

The players transition back to normal running whenever the airhorn or instrument sounds again.

5. Airhorn Sit

In this game, you also require just one airhorn (or instrument like a drum), and one cone per team.

Place the cone in the distance for each team, and they are going to run around this and back.

Give every person in the team a number, depending on how many players there are. If there are five players, then give them a number from 1 to 5.

The person with the airhorn is going to shout a number, e.g. 2. That person is going to stand up and run first. Off they go!

However, at any given point, the airhorn is going to be sounded, and that person is going to have to sit down. The person who is sitting is going to shout out the number this time - either 1, 3, 4 or 5 in the example. That person will start running, only to sit when the airhorn sounds again. Then it is their turn to shout the number.

Basically this process continues until all the team members have got round the cone and back, and are sitting in their original spaces once again.

6. Exercise Card Challenge

In this game, all you need are sets of cards with some pictures or instructions of exercises on them. Some examples might be, '5 star-jumps', '5 press-ups', '10 sit-ups', and other things like that.

You will need several sets of cards - as many sets as you have teams.

One player in each team is going to go and sit about fifty yards away from their team-mates, but facing back towards them. That person is going to be holding their team's pack of cards.

One player at a time will run towards that person. They will be given an exercise challenge from the pack of cards, for example, '5 squats.' They perform the exercise, and then run back to their team.

Then the next player goes, until all the team have had a go of the challenge.

7. Card Object Dash

Have a set of picture cards for each team. These will be images of a matching set of objects that you will also have. For example, it might be a 'ball', a 'key', a 'shoe', and a 'rope'. If you have four teams, you will have four of each object (along with the four sets of cards).

Split the players into relay teams, and it is important to have as many in each team as you have objects. So if you have five players in each team, have five objects.

The players sit in a physically distanced formation in lines. One player in each team is going to be in charge of the cards, and they sit at the front.

The objects for each team are going to be placed at different distances, in a straight line in front of the team. For example, the shoe might be ten yards in front of them, the key twenty yards, the rope thirty yards, and so on.

'Ready, set, go!' The player with the cards, shows the first card to the next person in the line. For example, it might be the 'ball.'

That player jumps up, runs to where the ball is, and circles around it. They run back and sit down. As soon as they get back, the person with the cards shows the next one in the pack (e.g. 'key') to the next person, and off they go towards that one.

The player holding the cards will go last. Whatever is the last card, they run off, circle round it, and come back. Whatever team are sat down first are the champions.

8. Card Objects Scatter

This is a harder version of the last game.

In this, instead of a team's objects being placed in a line, this time all the objects you have are scattered together in a massive mish-mash all over the place. They are accessed by all teams at the same time, and a runner can select whichever object they can see in the space. For example, get the 'shoe' card, and you can run to any shoe you can see and back.

There are more tactics in the this game, as players try to spot the corresponding object to the card that is closest to their position.

6

The Dutchman's Rope

A Dutchman's Rope is a length of rope, tied into a circle, with knots tied every seven feet.

Why seven feet? Because current standards suggest a minimum of six feet of separation for proper physical distancing and we like to exceed those minimum standards whenever possible.

Recommended physical distancing varies from country to country and may change as we move forward, so when preparing your own version of the Dutchman's Rope, please follow your local physical distancing guidelines.

Group members locate themselves at each of these knot positions which are a visual reminder to help them maintain appropriate physical distancing.

The Dutchman's Rope is typically placed on the ground, in a circle or a straight line for each of the following games.

How To Source A Dutchman's Rope

The Dutchman's Rope is such a simple idea that most camp professionals, teachers, trainers, facilitators and group leaders of all kinds can make one themselves using string, rope or any kind of cordage in about five minutes.

If you are not one of the do-it-yourself crowd, then you can also purchase one or more hand-crafted Dutchman's Ropes (50-feet-long with seven knots) from Training Wheels, Inc. (Training-Wheels.com) in the United States and RSVP Design (RSVPDesign.co.uk) in the United Kingdom. Each of these organizations also carry copies of an extensive booklet of Dutchman's Rope games, D-I-Y instructions and other resources for physically distanced play.

Choosing the color of your rope is important. This rope is going to spend a lot of time in the grass, on the ground, in the woods or on the athletic court, so choose a color that will hide the dirt.

After selecting your rope of choice, next comes the knots. There are a variety of acceptable knots, but I find that the larger they are, the easier they are to see and use.

A single overhand knot is too small for the Dutchman's Rope. At minimum use a figure eight knot or better still (and easier to tie), an overhand knot on a bight.

When your Dutchman's rope is up and running, you're ready to go.

1. Clap, Jump, Spin, Run

Who would guess that a game with just four actions could be so challenging?

Begin this action game by placing your Dutchman's Rope in a wide circle on the ground, and the players each stand at one knot. This is their 'home knot'. Leave one knot empty for this game.

The player starting the game faces in the direction of another player and while looking at them CLAPS in their direction.

This second player then JUMPS into the air and as they return to earth again, they point with one hand to another player who SPINS a 360. When they land, they point to a fourth player who runs from their current position to the location of the empty knot.

Then the game repeats itself, over and over again.

There's no penalty for making a mistake, but if a mistake happens, that player begins the sequence again from the beginning with CLAP.

Any group that can complete seven rounds of this game without making a mistake is indeed legendary. Good luck!

2. Fifty Ways to Cross a Circle

We borrowed this game from the world of improvisational comedy and theatre sports.

Begin by leaving one empty knot in the circle.

Start with the players standing at their 'home knot' position. Then the players are free to move, one at a time, whenever they like. Any player can cross the interior of the rope circle towards the empty knot, miming a unique mode of locomotion along the way.

They could, for example, row a canoe, or juggle, or carry a tray like a waiter or walk backwards.

The goal is to keep thinking of new, original ways to cross the circle without repeating someone else's technique.

3. The Story Stretch

One person in the group begins to tell a story that includes movements and motions. Each of the other members of the group replicate these movements.

The story could be about anything at all. It could include unicorns and witches, dragons and zombies. The more random the better. It could be about the day's activities, or about their birthday, a holiday they had, or whatever else.

After thirty to forty seconds, the next person continues the story, taking it in their own direction and adding physical movements and motions that actively engage the rest of the group in their story.

For example, 'One day, I went tip-toeing through the spooky forest.' (Everyone tip-toes in place). 'The trees where swaying.' (Everyone does swaying trees). 'Then I saw a unicorn galloping.' (Pretend to be galloping unicorns.)

For younger children you could just try to do one sentence per person at a time. For older ones, longer passages are possible.

In just a few minutes, you'll have a wonderfully alert and physically ready group of participants, and every one of them will have been given the opportunity to lead and be heard by the group.

4. Believe It Or Knot

This icebreaking activity is an opportunity for participants to share information about themselves as they sit near their home position knot on the Dutchman's Rope.

The information could be true or it could be false. I might say for example, that I have a twin brother.

Now the group will not know whether I have a twin brother or not, so they are allowed to ask three questions. In this case, I don't have a twin brother, but if someone asked me his name, I would make something up... such as Tim.

After three questions, the group must vote whether to believe me or not, after which I will tell them the truth.

One of the more unusual features of *Believe It or Knot* is that this is one activity that can be played multiple times as groups get to know each other.

Initially participants might only mention things that are generally known and not particularly personal or private, but as they get to know the other members of their group, many participants will begin to reveal interesting and more significant information.

5. The Morning Dance Party

This musical warm-up activity incorporates an element of leadership as well. Starting in a large circle around the rope, and accompanied by a source of music, everyone in the group has the opportunity to share a dance move, but only for about ten seconds.

The other group members replicate the dance movements of their leader.

Then the next person in the circle shares their dance movement.

We recommend that the group's leader provides an example of this style of dance leadership by going first in this activity.

There is a big difference between being a great dancer and a great dance leader.

By the way, our current favorite song for this particular activity is *Shut Up and Dance* by Walk the Moon.

6. The Story of Your Name

This is a particularly good game for the first day of a new term, camp, or club.

Begin this get-acquainted activity with everyone seated in a large circle around the rope.

The Story of Your Name is an opportunity for participants to share the story of how they came to have their name.

Perhaps they were named after an interesting relative or a friend of the family or someone famous. Include first, middle and last names as appropriate.

When each person finishes, ask them what they prefer to be called, and have the group practice calling them by their name of choice.

7. A Circle of Connection

A Circle of Connection is an outstanding way to gather the group together towards the end of a session or day.

Begin the activity with each person taking a knot position around the perimeter of a Dutchman's Rope.

Invite them to share some of the lessons they learned as a result of today's program or skills that they acquired. Invite them to continue speaking until another member of the group (just one) shares one of these comments, and then have that person stand at another knot position around the rope.

This second person then continues the activity, mentioning lessons learned or skills acquired until a third person joins the circle.

The process continues until everyone is standing around the perimeter of the rope.

8. The Little Labyrinth

For this activity, the Dutchman's Rope is placed in a spiral on the ground.

One players goes first, with the other's directing them. An object is placed at

THE DUTCHMAN'S ROPE

the center of the spiral, and the person who is 'on' has their eyes closed.

The challenge is for the single person to navigate the rope labyrinth with their eyes closed, retrieve the object that has been placed at the center, and return again without touching the rope at any time. This challenge can be performed with communication from an entire team or by working with a partner.

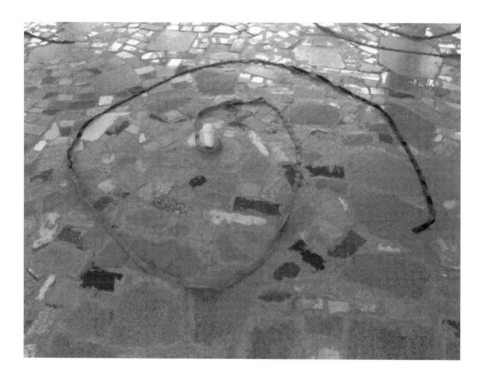

9. Human, Human, Zombie

This is a bit like Duck, Duck, Goose, just without the tagging element.

Everyone stands around the rope, with at least one spare knot being empty. One player is in the center of the rope circle.

That person goes around the inside of the circle, pointing one at a time at the other players, and saying, 'Human, Human, Human...' At any given moment they will point at someone and say, 'Zombie!'

The person in the middle will then run to the spare knot, run once around the circle, and get back to the spare knot, and end up once again in the center of the rope-circle. The zombie will be racing them! Whoever gets to the center of the circle first is the winner.

10. Countdown Switch

Everyone is seated near a knot, around the perimeter of the rope circle, leaving one empty knot location.

One player starts by saying 'ten' and the person next to them says, 'nine'. Continue counting down until the person that is 'zero' stands up and runs to the spare space.

This time they start with 'nine', the next person says 'eight', and keep going.

Every time you get to zero, they start the next round at one less than the round before. In the end there will be one person that starts at 'zero!' They will be the champion.

11. Food Reactions

In this game, the adult goes around the physically distanced circle, and tells everyone what food they are. Select about 5 different 'imaginary' foods, and go round saying something like, 'yoghurt, banana, burger, tomato, bread...'

Then one person is nominated to go in the middle of the circle.

That person is then going to try to say one of the food names three times in succession before anyone can interrupt them. For example, 'Yoghurt, yoghurt, yoghurt.'

Everyone on the 'yoghurt' team has to try to interrupt them by saying 'yoghurt' before they have said the third and final word.

The person in the middle keeps trying, until they successfully say one of the foods three times. Then someone from that food's 'team' takes their place.

7

Partner Games

Here is a selection of games where the players work with a partner. There is an emphasis on teamwork, fun, and interaction, all in the context of physical distancing.

1. Animal Noise Pairs!

This is a great ice-breaking game.

The players first spread out all around a wide space. Someone first goes round whispering to them what animal they are. There will be two of each animal.

So, for example, you might go round whispering, 'Donkey...cow...pig...chicken ...donkey...cow' etc. In the end you will have two of each animal.

The aim of the game is to find your matching partner. Everyone is going to start doing their animal noise, and walking round looking for someone doing the same.

When you find your partner, stand next to them (in a physically distanced way).

2. The Other Way

In this game, the players team up into partners and stand facing one another in a physically distanced way.

One player is the 'leader' to start with. They are going to point one of four directions – up, down, left or right. The other person must look in the opposite direction.

So, if the 'leader' points up, the other person has to immediately look straight down.

After the first go, you swap roles. The 'leader' now becomes the person looking at the other.

Keep going until one person makes a mistake (usually looking in the same way as the point).

3. One, Two, Three

This sounds simple on paper, but really gets them thinking.

The players stand in physically distanced pairings. One player says, 'One,' and then the next says, 'Two.' Then the first player says, 'Three,' and the next starts again at 'one.'

Keep going like this, alternating between the two players until someone makes a mistake.

4. Bang, Fizz, Pop

This is a variation of the 'One, Two, Three' game above, but in this game the numbers are substituted for the words, 'bang,' 'fizz' and 'pop'.

So players go, 'Bang...fizz...pop...bang...fizz...pop' and so on. Once again, this really gets them thinking.

You can extend it to five words to make it even more challenging. In this version it becomes, 'Bang, fizz, pop, whizz, pow!'

5. Shoe Toss Golf Partners

In this game, the players pair up into partners. Have about five cones or spots for each of the partners. The cones or spots will be arranged in a random array over the ground within about a ten yard radius from where the two partners are standing.

The player that will go first takes one of their shoes off. They will be standing, looking directly towards the mish-mash of cones on the floor. Then they close their eyes.

The idea of the game is that the person with one shoe off will throw their shoe at one of the cones. These are the golf holes. They must follow their throw, pick up their shoe wherever it landed, and keep on throwing the shoe until they make contact with one of the cones. Then they move onto another cone of their choice. The cones are the golf 'holes.'

The partner will be helping, and giving as many directions as possible.

You could potentially do this game against the clock. Or you could race against other teams. As soon as you have completed the five golf 'holes', then swap roles, and the next person takes off their shoe.

6. What Did You Say?

Children find this game hilarious.

Split the players into groups of three. Two stand about twenty yards away from each other, and facing directly at one another. The third person stands in between them, in a kind of 'piggy-in-the-middle' formation.

One of the players standing at the outside of the formation is going to start.

Pick a theme, for example films.

The person is going to shout out the name of any film of their choice to the person standing on the far side, behind the player in the middle. However, at the same time the person in the middle is going to be shouting and making noises to drown out what that person is saying!

They are only allowed to say the name of whatever it is once. Then the person on the other side must guess what they said. If they get it right, it's a point to the two players on the outside. Get it wrong, and the person in the middle scores a point.

Other topics could be things like food, vehicles, countries, or anything else you can think of.

You could have ideas written on cards for the players to get the ideas from, but it's probably just as easy to let them make them up.

7. Horse And Rider

This is a bit like Blind Man's Buff, only with lots of different rules that you can add to the mix.

Split the children into partners. One will stand in front of the other (in a physically distanced way), the other standing directly behind the first.

The partner at the front will now close their eyes. They are the 'horse'. The player behind them is the 'rider.'

The 'rider' will now direct the 'horse' around the playing area. There are lots of ways of playing, but you definitely could try some of these:
- Follow some kind of trail, maybe letters or numbers in order
- Have some cones that you are going to try to steer around
- Have the horse collect items, such as playing cards, along the way

8

Mindfulness Circle Games

Just as movement and action are crucial to children, so are moments of peacefulness and calm.

Brain-breaks and times to recharge are really important to the natural rhythm of learning. Our brains work well when receiving information, then processing it over a time period.

A constant stream of information does no-one any good.

A few fun mindfulness games thrown into sessions can work wonders. Here are a selection of simple games for all ages.

1. Raining On My Head

This is a simple guided visualization, as well as being a kind of self-massage.

The children sit in a physically distanced wide circle.

Tell the children that their fingers are now like the rain. Place their hands up above their heads, and use a pitter-patter movement of the fingers for the rain-drops.

Get them to close their eyes, and then lower their moving fingers onto their heads. Get them to visualize how their hair feels wet!

Then guide them that their fingers are pitter-pattering down their face, over their shoulders, down their sides, down their legs, and finishing on their feet.

Then sit back up and breathe deeply for a few moments. Ask them to imagine how the raining is steaming off them in the hot sun.

2. Hand Massages

One of the simplest massages that children can give to themselves is hand-massages.

There is a large network of nerves and muscles located in the hands, and so massaging this area can cause fast-working stress-relief.

Some simple hand-massages to try include:
   -Simply letting your hands and wrists go limp, and gently shaking them
   -Using your index finger of one hand to circle in the palm of your other
   -Use the fingers of one hand to gently circle on the top of your other hand

3. Pressure Points

There are a couple of simple pressure-point activities that children can try that are shown to relieve stress.

The simplest is to find the pressure-point in between your eyebrows. With your index finger, circle your finger on this spot.

The other pressure-point that is worth exploring is in the webbing of your hand, in between the thumb and the index finger. Press into the webbing with your index finger, and once again use a circular motion for about half a minute.

4. Bumble Bee Breathing

This is the first of three deep breathing games that I'm including here. This first one is the breathing game that is most suited to very young children.

The children pretend to be bumble bees! First practice doing a hum sound - 'hmmmm'.

Then they breathe in silently, and breathe out whilst doing a hum at the same time. Continue like this, silent in, and out with a hum.

5. Take 5 Game

This is a simple mindfulness game, where you focus your attention on one object (your hand). It is also a deep breathing game.

Deep breathing is the fastest way of calming us down quickly. It reduces our heart-rates, and lowers adrenaline.

For 'Take 5', invite children to show one hand, with all five fingers extended.

Then, with the index finger of one hand, they slowly run up one side of the thumb whilst breathing slowly in. Then they breathe out as they run down the other side of the thumb.

Then they breathe in whilst going up the index finger, out on the other side, and so on.

Continue like this, until they have competed the whole hand.

6. Breathe Our Colors

The idea of this game is to imagine a color that makes you feel happy.

Get the children to close their eyes, and breathe in deeply. Then, as they breathe out, tell the children to imagine the color they are thinking of is coming out of their mouths and filling the air around them. Keep breathing in and out, continuing to fill the space with the color.

This is a beautiful visualisation and deep breathing exercise combined.

7. Melting Moments

This is a guided meditation.

The children stand up, and pretend to be something that melts - for instance a snowman or a bar of chocolate.

Tell them to close their eyes, and really imagine that they are turning into whatever it is. If it is the snowman, they can feel the cold snow of their bodies, and that their nose has turned into a carrot.

Now the sun is coming out. Get them to imagine that they are starting to melt! They start shrinking, getting lower to the floor. In the end, they will be lying on the floor, having fully 'melted'.

9

Classic Game Variations

Many classic children's games can be easily adapted for physical distancing, including:
- Hide and Seek
- What's the Time Mr.Wolf?
- Capture The Flag
- Kick The Can
- Red Light, Green Light
- Mother May I?

And there are so many more obvious choices.

This chapter displays some classic games that children know and love, but switches them round a little to keep them engaging and fresh.

1. Rock Paper Scissors - Full Body

This is a rock paper scissors game played by up to six players at once.

The six players stand in a physically distanced circle facing each other. The main idea of the game is that you use your whole body to create the rock paper scissors movements - arms up straight for paper, one arm and leg straight out for scissors, and curl up for rock.

Everyone in the team plays Rock Paper Scissors – 'Rock, Paper, Scissors… Shoot!' They each show their particular big movement – e.g. 'scissors.'

If all three possibilities are shown, then you just go again.

However, if just two are shown, then you will have some people that are the winners, and some that are out. For example, if some children show scissors, and the others show paper, then the paper has lost. Those children sit down.

Then you just go again with the children that are still standing. In the end you will have a champion. Then play the game again.

2. Rock Paper Scissors Rope Train

To play this game, you need a rope with some kind of markings about every two yards (a Dutchman's rope would be ideal).

To play this game, one child starts as the 'train driver.' The others (probably up to about ten), are waiting in a physically distanced line at the station.

The driver goes around the 'track', pulling the rope behind them. It's good if this is quite a small area to speed up the game. It could, for example, be a circle of cones that are about ten yards in diameter.

Then the driver approaches the first person waiting in the station line. The driver stops a few yards from them, and they play one round of rock, paper, scissors.

Whoever wins is the driver of the train, the other one becomes the 'carriage', and goes behind the 'driver.' The carriage holds the rope at the first marking after where the train is holding it.

Off they both go now, around the track once more, before the driver plays rock, paper, scissors with the next person in the line.

That person, in turn, becomes either the driver or another carriage. In the end, everyone is driving around behind the final train driver.

3. Charades – Pick A Theme

This is a much simpler version of the classic game, charades.

You pick a theme in this, and the person who is 'it' is going to pretend to be something from the theme.

For example, the theme might be vehicles, and the person who is 'it' might pretend to be riding a bike, or a scooter, or a plane, or driving a car.

Some topics to choose from include:

- Superheroes
- Vehicles
- Sports

4. Charades – Physical Activities

This is another good and simple charades game, that can be done by children probably from quite a young age upwards.

One child, standing in front of the group, mimes some kind of physical activity. The other children try to guess what they're doing.

Some good examples might be:

- Brushing their teeth
- Running
- Eating something
- Swimming
- Skiing
- Throwing a ball
- Kicking a ball
- Blowing up a balloon
- Throwing a frisbee or a baseball
- Playing cricket
- Throwing (and catching) a boomerang

It's as simple as that.

5. Simon Says Variations

Of course pretty much everyone knows the classic rules of 'Simon Says', and here are some variations on the classic game.

Begin first with the usual version of the game, before expanding to some of these:

Fast Version

Continue the game with more challenging and faster movements and motions.

Do As I Say, Not As I Do

Continue the game, but follow a command with the opposite movement, such as: *put your right hand up, Simon Says put your right hand down.*

Do The Opposite Of What I Say

For example, 'Simon Says wave your hand' (whilst patting your back).

6. Twister (Without A Mat)

This is an incredibly fun game that encourages challenging physical movements.

The players spread out across a wide area, giving themselves plenty of room to move wherever they are.

The facilitator is going to give them lots of moves to perform on the spot. It could be things like, 'Put your left foot in front of the other.' 'Touch the ground with your left hand in front of your left foot.' 'Put your right hand behind your right foot.'

Keep going until the players can no longer perform the moves without falling over.

10

Active Physical Distancing Games

Here are a selection of games that get everyone moving and active.

1. Stop, Go!

This is a game of movement, listening, and thinking all combined.

Players walk round a wide space. The facilitator gives out several commands, and these increase in difficulty as the game progresses.

Start with 'stop', and 'go'. When you say 'go', the players walk around the space in any direction. When the facilitator says 'stop' then the players stop. Pretty simple so far.

However, the first way to mix things up, is to make the words mean their opposite - so 'stop' becomes 'go', and 'go' becomes 'stop'. Have a go of this.

Introduce more commands. They could be 'forwards' and 'backwards', 'left' and 'right', 'jump' and 'clap', for example.

You can also try these versions of the games:
   -Do the same and say the opposites
   -Do the opposite and say the same
   -Do the opposite and say the opposite

A real brain teaser!

2. Animal Pack

First, have the players spread out over a wide area.

The facilitator is going to move around the group whispering to each person in turn what animal they are. Pick two animals, and have the group roughly (but randomly) split in two.

Have some physically distanced cones or markers placed in two areas of the space - these are for the two teams of animals to stand on when they have teamed up.

Say, 'Go!' And the players begin moving around the space. They all move in the manner of the animal that they have been given. Some good animals to choose are:
  -Monkeys
  -Elephants
  -Snakes
  -Tigers

But be creative! The idea is that the animals should be able to find other players that are clearly the same animals as themselves, and move as a group towards one of the team-areas.

3. The Invisible Obstacle Course

This physical warm-up activity takes place in an imaginative environment. Think of it as an imaginary form of Parkour.

Begin in cohort groups of six to eight people. A volunteer leads the entire group to the first element of an imaginary obstacle course. After describing and then demonstrating the proper technique for crossing their imaginary obstacle, all remaining members of the group follow their leader, while maintaining appropriate physical distancing.

Then another member of the group takes the leadership role and leads the group through the next obstacle.

A variety of imaginary obstacles are possible. Climbing trees or infinite ladders, rope swings, swimming through giant waves in the ocean, jumping over ravines and crevasses, lifting heavy loads, juggling small animals, etc. The elements of each obstacle course are limited only by the imagination of the group.

4. Hidden Treasure

Before players arrive, hide a small object somewhere in the available space. It might be a coin, a small toy, or something similar.

Then, when players arrive, invite them to search for the object.

Whenever they find it, they must say nothing, but come and sit back down in the original space (in a physically distanced way).

This is a good game for looking around at others, and spotting their reactions and behavior.

5. Jumping Jacks

Players first stand in a space in a wide playing area. This is a jumping game with a difference.

Tell the group first that you want them to 'Say what I say, and do what I say'.

Give some commands involving different types of jumps. For example, 'Jump forward', 'jump backwards', 'jump left', 'jump right.'

When they have had a good go of that, then mix up the difficulty. Now say, 'Say the opposite of what I do, and do what I say.'

So now, if you say, 'jump right,' everyone will jump right, while saying, 'Jump left'.

After they have had a good go of that, increase the difficulty yet again. This time say, 'Say what I say, do the opposite of what I say.'

Another tricky option is, 'Say the opposite of what I say, do the opposite of what I say.'

6. Count Six

For this arm-waving challenge, organize your participants into groups of six, then demonstrate the following motions with the right arm.

Right arm straight up. Count 1.
Right arm straight out, parallel to the ground. Count 2.
Right arm straight down, at your side. Count 3.

> Right arm straight up again. Count 4.
> Right arm straight out again. Count 5.
> Right arm straight down again. Count 6.

Then introduce the left arm movement.

> Left arm straight up. Count 1.
> Left arm straight down, at your side. Count 2.
> Left arm straight up. Count 3.
> Left arm straight down. Count 4.
> Left arm straight up. Count 5.
> Left arm straight down. Count 6.

Now the challenge is to combine movements with both arms at the same time.

Ready? 1, 2, 3, 4, 5, 6!

Once the laughter has subsided, allow each group four minutes to perfect their arm motions by working together, then ask them to demonstrate their ability to perform this task with absolute perfection.

7. Count to Five Race

To begin this challenging activity, organize your participants into groups of five.

Have a wide circle of cones spread out in the playing area. You need at least as many cones as you have teams of five (and a couple of extra cones is not a problem).

The teams go and lie down in a physically distanced way, each near one of the cones. They close their eyes.

This is now a race. Ready…set…go!

With their eyes still closed, the players in each team must try to count to five. Each player can only say one number, and if you say two numbers at the same time, you have to start again at '1.'

When a team successfully gets to 'five', they are going to jump up, run to a vacant cone in the circle, lie down near it in a physically distanced way again, and begin the same process.

They have to do the same game five times by which time they have completed the task.

11

I'm In Games

The book *Find Something To Do* (ISBN 978-0-9882046-0-7) by Jim Cain contains more than a dozen *I'm In Games*.

The challenge of these games is for individual members of the group to demonstrate to the leader that they are 'in the know'. That is, they have figured out the mystery of the game and can reveal that knowledge to the leader without giving away the secret.

These games are particularly ideal for children over the age of about ten. Also, bear in mind you can play them several times before giving the secret of the game away. There is no need for everyone to 'get' it first time round.

1. Silly Tilly Williams

In this game, the leader shares a few innocuous things that Silly Tilly likes and other things that she does not.

For example, Silly Tilly Williams likes puppies but not dogs. She likes books but not magazines. She likes tennis, but not hockey. She likes dinner but not lunch.

At this point, other members of the group begin to brainstorm various things that Silly Tilly might or might not like. Does she like bicycles? No, she does not. What about bookstores or libraries? Yes to bookstores, no to libraries. Pizza and spaghetti? Yes to both.

The secret of Silly Tilly Williams is that she likes things with double letters. Kittens but not cats. Doors but not windows. Summer not winter.

2. I Can Pogo

Another favorite 'I'm in' game is 'I Can Pogo'.

In this game, the leader mentions three unique places where they can pogo, followed with great conviction by the phrase, I CAN POGO as they point both thumbs at themselves. A demonstration would be a bit like:

> Okay. I can pogo on the moon.
> I can pogo on the basketball court.
> I can pogo on the Fourth of July...
> I CAN POGO!

As the individual members of the group attempt to demonstrate their awareness of the game, by mentioning three places followed by the phrase, I CAN POGO, the leader will then verify their claim, or sadly remark, "nope sorry, you can't pogo."

The secret of this *I'm In Game*, is that before stating the three locations, the speaker has to say 'okay.' If you don't say okay, you can't pogo!

3. My Grandfather's Music Box

'My Grandfather's Music Box' is certainly the most challenging 'I'm In Game' we have listed here, and also by far the most difficult game in this book.

You say, 'My Grandfather gave me a music box. It is one of my most treasured keepsakes, but it doesn't always work. I discovered, however, that if you put the right things into the box, it plays beautiful music. What would you like to put into the music box?'

Next, offer your audience examples of what you might place into the box.

If, for example, I put a doorknob into the box, it plays beautiful music. I could even put an entire door into the box, and that would work. If I put my Mom into the music box, nothing happens. If I put my Dad in, same thing.

Ah, but if I put my Father into the music box, it plays beautiful music. If I put in a chair nothing happens, but if I put in a sofa, it plays twice as nice. Now, what would you like to put into the music box?

At this point, the members of your group will begin suggesting different objects to be placed into the music box.

The secret of this 'I'm In Game' is that the name of the object being placed into the music box must contain the letters of at least one of the words DO, RE, ME, FA, SO, LA, TI, DO. A doorknob for example, contains the letters DO, so it qualifies. So does a dictionary (TI). And the reason a sofa plays twice as nice? Because it contains both SO and FA!

4. Polar Bears And Ice Holes

You'll need five dice for this particular game. To begin, the facilitator rolls all five dice at the same time, then asks the group to count the numbers of ice holes and the number of polar bears revealed. It is important to note that you can have an ice hole without a polar bear, but you cannot have a polar bear without an ice hole.

The challenge of this game is to determine what features on the dice constitute an ice hole, and what features are the polar bears. Playing multiple times helps the members of the group try different reasoning in the hopes of discovering the solution.

In this case, ice holes refer to the central dot on any die face, of which there are three. On the one, three and five faces. Polar Bears are the dots surrounding any of these central dots, on the three and five die faces. The two, four and six die faces of any dice do not reveal anything at all.

5. Cowboys Around The Campfire

This game is a variation of the polar bear game above.

In 'Cowboys Around The Campfire', the central dot on any die face is the campfire and any dots surrounding these central dots are the cowboys.

One of the more important things about playing *I'm In Games* with any group is never to use this activity as a way to separate or divide the group (those that know vs. those that do not). Instead, try to introduce the game, play for a few minutes, then stash the game away for a while before revisiting it again.

And don't be in a hurry to reveal the solution. Allowing the members of your group the opportunity to figure things out for themselves is a valuable lesson in perseverance and tenacity.

12

Challenge Games

Here are a selection of fun challenges that involve all sorts of memory, teamwork, and thinking skills. They take place in a range of physically distanced contexts.

1. Breakfast Memory Challenge

This is a memory game that also acts as a kind of ice-breaker.

The players sit in a physically distanced circle. The easy form of the game is that the first person in the circle says what they had for breakfast, e.g. 'For breakfast we had cornflakes.'

Next person in the circle restates what the first person in the circle said, but then also adds to this. So they might say, 'For breakfast we had cornflakes, and Apple Jacks.'

In the easy version, each player just says the one person's breakfast that came before them, and their own.

In the hard version, the players keep building on what has been said. So the fifth person, for example, will have to remember the previous four breakfasts, plus add their own.

This game could also be played with different topics, such as:
 -Favorite pastimes
 -Favorite sports
 -Favorite food

2. Seven Folds

Consider this challenge as a form of extreme origami.

Take any index card or piece of paper (any size, shape or color), and fold it in half. That's one.

Now fold it in half again. That's two.

And again, and again, and again until you have made seven folds. Can you do it?

The simple task of folding a piece of paper is easy at the start, but becomes more difficult with each additional fold.

If practice makes perfect, why doesn't folding get easier with each fold rather than more difficult?

What happens between the fifth, sixth and seventh folds that is different than between the second, third and fourth folds?

Does the thickness of the paper have anything to do with the difficulty of this challenge?

Does the original size of the paper matter?

Would it be possible to fold the paper in half a different way, to make this task easier?

3. Number Spot Race

For this game you need some kind of rubber spots with numbers written on from 1 to 6 (you could also use paper plates or sequential playing cards). You will need one set of these for each team.

Split the players into teams of six. Every team needs quite a wide space just for them, and the spots or plates are scattered in a random array around that area. Then get the teams to number themselves from 1-6.

This is now a speed challenge. Quite simply, on saying, 'Go!' the players run around their space, and try to find the number that corresponds to them. The first team to all be standing on their spots are the champions.

4. Action Story Challenge

This is a group storytelling activity, but with some actions and key-words thrown in.

Stand in a physically distanced circle, and the facilitator explains that they are about to tell a story. However, in the story there will be some words to listen out for. If you hear one of the words, then there is an action to do.

For example, one word might be 'giant'. Hear that, and you have to stomp like a giant on the spot, swinging your arms.

Other words might be 'snake' (lie on the floor and slither), and 'happy' (do a happy dance).

Then tell the story, throwing in some of the action-words now and then. The children could add their own ideas to the story, or suggest action-words with associated movements.

5. The Story Listening Challenge

Here is a fun game that requires players to think and talk on their feet!

Begin by writing a single word on a dozen or more index cards. Nouns are traditionally useful words for this activity, but you can also add additional words of importance, such as adjectives, verbs, mission statement words, character building phrases, and more. Be sure to use large index cards (5x8) and print the words in large block letters.

Then distribute one card to each member of your audience and invite each person to take a seat in a circle of physically distanced chairs facing outward. Once seated, invite everyone to hold their card so that anyone passing in front of them can easily read the word shown.

The facilitator can demonstrate this activity by taking the role as storyteller the first time.

The storyteller begins by walking around the circle, telling a story they make up as they go along. Of course, all stories begin with the phrase *once upon a time.* Every time the facilitator (storyteller) mentions a word printed on one of the cards, the person holding that card stands up and follows the facilitator as they walk around the outside perimeter of the group.

The storyteller should intentionally look at the various cards they pass as they walk around the circle and attempt to incorporate as many of these words as they can during the telling of their tale.

After what is likely to be a random story (which is part of the fun), the storyteller concludes with the phrase *and they all lived happily ever after, the end!* At which point everyone tries to find a seat, including the storyteller (while maintaining physical distance). The one person without a seat becomes the storyteller for the next round.

After a few rounds, invite everyone to write a new word on their index card, and then continue the game. You can even encourage participants to write words specific to a historical event, children's book, quotation, mission statement, vision statement, camp theme, core values or other useful words.

This style of impromptu story telling is a great way to practice public speaking. Some stories are hilarious and some storytellers manage to get almost everyone in the circle on their feet during the telling of their tale.

6. Team Ordering

Split children up into teams of about 10 for this game.

Have a set of numbers from 1 to 10 for each team (this could just be pieces of A4 paper with numbers written on). The numbers will be folded in half, so the players can't see what number the paper has on it.

The players in each team select one number each, and then stand in a long physically distanced line. You could stand on rubber spots to make the distancing issue easier.

Everyone opens out their number to see what they've got.

The idea is to get into order from 1-10 - but here's the catch. Only two numbers can swap at any given moment.

The players need to swap their way to being in the right sequence. It takes a while to get their heads around this.

7. Tightrope Walk

Tightrope walks can be done with many different types of difficulty. They can include:
   -Walking along lines on the floor
   -You can create an impromptu tightrope with masking tape or sidewalk chalk
   -Walking along a long rope in a line placed on the floor
   -Walking along a long rope that curves in different directions
   -Create an 'obstacle-course' of different ropes to balance across

-Holding a pool noodle in either hand, and getting helped to balance

-Walking along a rope, whilst holding a long pole being helped by two teammates on either end of it

-Using a rope tied between two trees, and once again holding a long pole

13

Fun Zoom Games Across The Curriculum

In any virtual session, there are huge benefits to injecting fun, humor, and just moments where the children can interact with each other on a purely human level.

These games are all focussed massively on that - interaction with others, and developing social connection.

All of these games are relatively quick to play, and so they can be thrown into other sessions or lessons, to break things up, and strengthen interest and engagement.

Another advantage of all these games below is that the vast majority could also be played in the 'real' world, with players sitting in an appropriately physically distanced way.

1. Joey Tribbiani

There is an episode in the TV Show 'Friends' where Joey (Matt Le-Blanc's character), puts on all of his roommate Chandler's clothes.

So – here's the challenge (best played with a child's computer in their bedroom, or someplace where they have access to plenty of clothes), players have two minutes to put on as many layers of clothing as they can!

2. Detective Game

In this game, one player is first selected to be the 'detective'.

That person will close their eyes. Hold up the name-card of one other person in the group so that everyone can see who it is on the screen. This person is the secret 'leader'.

This person will start by doing some kind of repeating action, and the others will follow. For example, they might clap their hands. Everyone else will copy.

Then the 'detective' opens their eyes, as the others are all doing the move. At any given moment, the 'leader' will start doing a new repeated move (like patting their head), and all the others will copy.

The 'detective' will be trying to spot who is leading the moves. The game keeps going with different moves, until the 'detective' works out who it is.

3. Rock Paper Scissors Olympics

One person, the leader, is 'on'. Everyone else is competing against this person.

Together, they all go, 'Rock…paper…scissors…shoot!' and show the hand signal for rock, paper or scissors. If you are beaten by the person who is 'on', then you are out. If you get the same, or you win, then you keep going.

In the end there is often a 'head to head' between two people. Who will win!?

4. Silent Animal Charades

This is the easiest version of charades, ideal for all ages.

One child is 'on' and pretends to be an animal (with their mute button on). Everyone else guesses what they are.

So, for example, if they were an elephant, they might gesture that they have big ears, a long trunk, and be stamping on the spot.

5. It's Your Choice

In this game, participants are asked to make a choice. Explanations are not required, but invited. For example, which are you more like - a sparkler or a firecracker?

You can get the children to all respond at the same time with a gesture. So, as an example, say, 'Which are you more like? A beach (shown by one horizontal arm), or a mountain (create a triangle with two arms).'

Let the children think in their own time and respond.

Here are a few examples of questions for this activity. Are you more like:
   -*Bookstores or Libraries*
   – *Words or Numbers*
   – *PC or Mac*
   – *Car or Truck*

- Odd or Even Text Message or Voice Message
- Software or Hardware
- A Firecracker or a Sparkler Dine In or Carry Out
- Professional Sports or Amateur Sports
- Walking or Running
- Window or Aisle
- Weekday or Weekend
- Star Wars or Star Trek
- Day or Night

6. 1, 2, 3, Look! Numbers

One person is 'on'.

Everyone else closes their eyes. They put a number of fingers up on their hand, for example, 'three.'

Without being seen, the person who is 'on' also puts a quantity of fingers up on their hand.

Then everyone says, '1, 2, 3, look!' They open their eyes. If you have the same number of fingers up as the person on the screen, you win!

Repeat a few times, before changing the person that is 'on'.

7. 1, 2, 3, Look! Emotions

This game is similar to the '1, 2, 3, look! Numbers,' game.

This time everyone pulls an emotion face when their eyes are closed. They might pretend to be happy, sad, or cross, for example. The person who is 'on' does one of these faces also.

'1, 2, 3, look!' and open your eyes to see if you've got the same face as the person that is 'on'.

8. Can't Laugh Challenge

A very simple idea behind this one. One child is 'on', and they do everything they can to make everyone else laugh. If you laugh you are out.

Some strategies to try include doing silly faces, making funny noises, telling jokes, and all that kind of thing.

9. Guess The Object

The idea of this game is that one person is 'on'. They are going to show just a tiny bit of an object. This is best done up close to the camera.

For example, you might show the top of the ear of a toy bear.

Everyone else tries to guess what the object is.

You can also do this game as a describing game. One person simply describes the object that cannot be seen on-screen.

10. Mystery Song

One person is the focus of attention. They are going to put their mute button on, and then sing a song. They could be playing the music in the background, or just singing it (whichever is easier – as no one can hear them anyway).

Everyone else tries to guess what song they are singing. First person to type the correct song title in the cat feature, wins!

12. Draw A Picture With Eyes Closed

There are many drawing activities you can try on Zoom, but this one really stands out. You'll need a blank piece of paper and a pencil for each player.

There are different ways of playing the game.

One way is that the adult describes what to draw, and everyone has a go of doing that with their eyes closed. It's good to include a few different features in the picture.

So you might say, 'Draw a tree. Under it is a flower. There is a bird in the sky next to a cloud. A boy is on a slide.'

Another way of playing the game is a bit like pictionary. Pick a theme, for example 'vehicles'. One person is 'it'. They have to pick a vehicle in their head, and then draw it with their eyes closed. They show everyone the picture, and they all try to guess.

13. Draw A Picture With Paper On Your Head

Want to make things even harder - then why not try drawing a picture with the paper on your head!

They find looking at everyone else's picture truly hysterical.

14. Do As I Say, Not As I Do

This is a classic listening game that works really well in the virtual world.

One child is 'on'. They are going to be telling the other children how to move, but trying to trick them at the same time by doing different movements themselves. The others have to do what they say, not what they do.

So they might pat their head, while saying, 'Clap your hands.' The players have to clap their hands (not pat their head). Or, 'Put your hands up high,' as they put theirs down low.

Doing this game at high-speed also increases the difficulty, with multiple ideas coming thick and fast.

15. Type One Word Game

One person is 'on' for this one.

That person is going to say a sentence, for example, 'The dog went up the...' They miss the last word out. The person that has said the sentence will know what the missing word is. They might even write it down out of sight to avoid any cheating.

Everyone else is going to try to fill in the missing word, by typing their answer into the group chat box. Who got it right?

For this game, you can also do:
　–One person asks questions, and the others try to answer them. For example, 'What is the capital of France?
　–Rhyming words, e.g. 'Write a word that rhymes with 'cat'.'
　–Play 'I Spy' or similar games, e.g. 'I spy something that begins with 't'.'

14

Active Virtual Games

> *As the bottom gets numb-er, the brain gets dumber!*

Marcia L. Tate

> *Movement is the door to learning.*

Paul Dennison

For decades parents have been concerned about the amount of time their children spend in front of the television. However, now it is many of those parents themselves who are watching a screen for hours and hours each day as they work from home, interact with family, and adapt to the 'new normal'.

Add to that total increased screen time for at-home schooling, and suddenly our entire population is spending a major portion of each day sedentary, watching a screen. If we're not careful, we're all going to end up looking like the inhabitants from the spaceship in the movie WALL-E.

It's no surprise then that many people are looking for creative ways to incorporate more movement and activity into their virtual learning.

Here are a selection of games that can be played during virtual learning sessions that are active, physical, and fun. These are all super-quick, and can break up your sessions with much needed moments to re-energize.

All these are fun Physical Education games that keep children moving in imaginative ways on the spot, with no requirement to move around the room.

1. Extra Sensory Perception (ESP)

Invent three movements and demonstrate these for the group. For example, a cowboy twirling a lariat above their head, a camp counselor spelling out YMCA and a college athlete throwing a fast ball from the pitcher's mound.

Then assign everyone a partner (or have them find their own from the field currently available on their screen).

The challenge of this activity is to activate your ESP, that is, your extra-sensory perception - the ability to read your partner's mind.

On the count of three, everyone displays one of the three movements previously described, but not at random. Choose the movement that you think your partner is about to do. Ready?

1, 2, 3!

Get the same move? You've activated your ESP!

ESP is a very brief way of getting your audience up and moving, even if only for a minute or two. You can play multiple rounds of the activity, and switch partners.

2. Figures Of Eight

The simple idea behind this game is that the players are going to be standing in front of their screen and attempt to make a figure of eight with different parts of their body.

For example, you can make an eight with:
- Your finger
- Elbow
- Knee
- Foot
- Head
- Butt
- Belly
- Your eyes
- Your tongue

As a further extension, players could sign their name using various body parts.

3. Dance Counting

You need some kind of dice for this one, and some sort of loud pumping disco music - ideally something without any words.

Get the children to stand up in front of their computer, then teach them a simple dance routine. It is probably best to stick to about four moves to start with. For example, arms to the right, arms to the left, arms up high, arms down low.

Now roll the dice. Whatever number you get, you are going to do that number of moves to the music.

So roll a 3, and you go - arms to the right three times, arms to the left three times, etc.

Keep rolling the dice, and experimenting with different numbers.

4. Bob Up

The children sit down to being this game.

The idea here is that you ask the children a question. If the answer for them is 'yes' then they jump up on their feet, and then sit back down straight away. This is the 'bob up' movement.

You might ask them, 'Do you like tomatoes?' The ones that do will bob up.

Ways of extending the game are:
    -Children ask the questions
    -Bob up and do a funky pre-designated move, such as do a funny dance or a silly face

5. Animal Copy Cat

One child is 'on' for this game. They are the 'cat' that everyone else is going to try to copy.

This child then moves, on the spot, like some kind of animal. For example, like an elephant. They swing their trunk and stamp their feet.

The person that is 'on' will switch things up about every twenty seconds, by trying out a different animal.

Everyone else tries to copy.

Then switch to someone else being 'on'. They try a new animal.

A variation of this game, is that the person who is 'on' can also say 'freeze' at any given moment. Freeze in your animal pose. Anyone that they see moving is 'out.'

6. Transformers

Lots of children are passionately excited by vehicles and transformers, and this is another activity that can be done more or less on the spot.

The children are now transformers. They get to shape-shift into all sorts of vehicles. Nominate either a child or the adult to be 'on' and decide which vehicles to pick.

Some good ideas for vehicles are:
   i) *Helicopter* – arms spinning round above your head
   iii) *Train* – using 'chugging arms'
   iv) *Racing cars* – running in place fast
   v) *Monster truck* – make yourself as big as possible, and chug on the spot
   vi) *Plane* – arms out, 'swooping' (on the spot)

7. Mr Men/Little Miss Game

The simple idea of this is that the players pretend to be different characters from the Little Miss or Mr Men books. They do the movements on the spot.

Some good ones to try include:

Mr Tall – walk on the spot as high as possible

Mr Grumpy – stamp with an angry face

Little Miss Tiny – Curl up like a ball

If they can think of their own ideas then great! If not, just come up with some as the adult, and maybe demo some simple ways of moving like that character.

8. Child-Friendly Yoga

Incorporating a few of the easier yoga movements in virtual learning is a sure-fire way to boost engaging, and incorporate mindfulness into your session.

The Alphabet Stretch invites participants to use their bodies to create each letter of the alphabet in a smoothly flowing succession, from A to Z. Participants can move at their own speed, and define their own movements.

Household Yoga consists of slow movements created to mimic household activities, such as reaching high up on the top shelf to retrieve a box of cereal, or simultaneously washing a window with one hand while stirring a pot of soup with the other.

The participants can invent their own moves. The activity continues until everyone has shared at least one household yoga movement.

Child-friendly animal yoga moves can be used with children of all ages. Some good examples are:

Giraffe Pose

Stand with one foot in front of the other. Reach up high with one arm above you (this is the giraffe's neck). Then bend slowly down, touching your front foot with the arm that had been high up, before rising again to the original position.

Turtle Pose

Lie on your back, with your knees pulled into your chin. Rock gently forwards and backwards like a turtle in its shell.

Seal Pose

Lie on your front, with your hands flat on the floor under your shoulders. Push upwards until your arms are straight, arching your back.

15

101 Additional Physically Distanced Activities

Juggling · Jogging · Yoga · Journaling · Line Dancing · Simon Says · Sudoku · Suguru · Crossword Puzzles · Storytelling · Exploring Nature · Arts & Crafts · Reading · Practice Meditation & Mindfulness · Multi-Player Video Games · Stargazing · Mad Libs · Map & Compass Courses · Playing the Guitar · Tongue Twisters · Riddles · Qi Gong · Tai Chi · Origami · String Figures · Composing a Poem or a Haiku · 1 Minute Mysteries · Solitaire · Painting · Paper Airplanes · Boomerangs · Archery · Photographic Scavenger Hunt · Ultimate Facial Mask Competition · Hula Hoops · Cycling · Paddle Boarding · Kayaking · Frisbee Golf · Baton Twirling · Geocaching · Calisthenics · Gardening · Show Your Gratitude · Calligraphy · Watch the Sunrise · Baking · Cooking · Photography · Drum Circles · Eating by Candlelight · Make a list of all the things you want to do when the pandemic is over · Whittling or Wood Carving · Surfing · Target Shooting · Virtual Activities including Escape Rooms and Scavenger Hunts · Fishing · Outdoor Cooking · Hiking & Backpacking · Walking · Jumping Rope · Building a Sand Castle · Making and Flying Kites · Building a Snowman or an Ice Carving · Writing a Postcard to a Friend · Mountain Biking · Hopscotch · Trying a New Food · Inventing a Non-Contact Handshake or Greeting · Read an e-book · Make a Snow Angel · Building an Inuksuit · Tennis · Translating a Word, Phrase or Message into a Foreign Language · Zumba · Hosting a Fashion Show · Having a Trivia Party · Starting a Diary · Drawing · Creating a Comic Strip · Writing a Thank You Note · Parkour · Creating a Flash Mob Dance Sequence · Scrapbooking · Bird Watching · Piloting a Drone · Blogging · Songwriting · Quilting · Knitting · Carpentry · Skipping Stones · Yo-Yoing · Snorkeling · Scuba Diving · Pilates · Extreme Ironing · Skateboarding & Mountainboarding · Learn Magic · Start a Collection · Learn How to Solve a Rubik's Cube · Create Temporary Art ·

As if there weren't enough physically distanced ideas in this book already, we thought we would go all out and present you with 101 more options.

Although there's lots of things you can't do whilst physically distancing, there really is so much that you can do.

A Little More Depth

We realize that simply mentioning an activity does not provide all the information necessary to incorporate that activity into your school, camp, social gathering or family event, so here's more of an explanation of each...

1. Juggling – type 'learn to juggle' on YouTube for several video tutorials. Be sure to supply participants with their own juggling balls or scarves.

2. Jogging or Trail Running – an excellent way to improve physical fitness and cardiovascular health. Stagger the starting times to help maintain physical distancing.

3. Yoga – Be sure to stand where participants can easily see you. Spread out. My favorite yoga video is here: YouTube.com/watch?v=d0ohbKdnEhw.

4. Journaling - Start by creating your own book, or get a blank book from www.barebooks.com.

5. Line Dancing – The Cupid Shuffle and the Cha Cha Slide are popular, but you can find both music and instructions for many more dances online at YouTube.com.

6. Simon Says – Turn this popular children's game into a whole-camp activity, just be sure everyone can see and hear the leader. Download Scott Gurst's outstanding document on leading Simon Says at:www.teamworkandteamplay.com/SimonSays.

7. Sudoku – Photocopy Sudoku puzzles and hold competitions for speed and accuracy. You can download tons of free Sudoku puzzles, for beginners, intermediates and experts at: KrazyDad.com.

8. Suguru – Another style of number puzzle. You can download tons of free Suguru puzzles for beginners, intermediates and experts at: KrazyDad.com.

9. Crossword Puzzles – There are plenty of online sources for free crossword puzzles, including Puzzles.USAToday.com.

10. Storytelling – Encourage your staff and program participants to share stories, especially ones with inspiration and hope.

11. Explore Nature – Take a walk in the woods, look for signs of wild animals, learn the names of every plant you discover, take a deep breath and describe what the great outdoors smells like.

12. Arts & Crafts – create something wonderful, but package each craft in a do-it-yourself kit, so that no resources are shared.

13. Read – collect a variety of books that will engage and inspire your audience and invite them to take one.

14. Practice Meditation and Mindfulness – Search for Internet resources and

learn about these two techniques. Perfect for reducing stress and anxiety (which can happen during a global pandemic).

15. Multi-Player Video Games – Acquaint yourself with this program possibility, just remember you can also play Scrabble, Five Crowns and a host of other board and family games online too.

16. Stargazing – Learn about star constellations and which planets are visible in your area.

17. Mad Libs (created by Leonard Stern and first shared publicly in 1958). You can play this game with any group, and download free printable versions of the game at: MadLibs.com/printables/.

18. Map & Compass Courses – Encourage discovery in your neighborhood by creating a map and compass course. You can find more information online, and at: NCACBSA.org/wp-content/uploads/2018/08/2018-Philmont-Training-III-7.2-MapCompass-101.pdf.

19. Learn to play the guitar. You can even take music lessons online.

20. Tongue Twisters – Start with the Dr. Seuss book, *Fox in Socks* and then progress to the website Tongue-Twister.net where you can find over 3600 tongue twisters in 118 languages.

21. Riddles – Question: What gets wetter the more it dries? Answer: A towel.

22. Qi Gong – This ancient form of daily exercise is a simple way to start each day, building strength, flexibility and balance. YouTube.com has online videos and you can find out more from the National Qigong Association at NQA.org.

23. Tai Chi – A movement-oriented form of daily exercise, with hundreds of movements and styles.

24. Origami – There are hundreds of paper-folding possibilities out there (Origami-Instructions.com) including online videos at YouTube.com.

25. String Figures – A traditional story-telling art in many cultures. You can find dozens of possibilities at StringFigures.info.

26. Composing a Poem or a Haiku. Haiku are three-line poems with five, seven and five syllables in each line. For example: *Some Haiku are odd. They can make no sense at all. I'll have a root beer.* Type the phrase poetic forms into your web browser and you'll find over a hundred forms of poetry.

27. One Minute Mysteries – You walk into a deserted cabin, in the middle of a blizzard. There is a fireplace, a lantern, and a single match. Which one do you light first? Answer: the match!

28. Solitaire – Discover the rules for Solitaire and other card games for one at CardGameHeaven.com and more fun things to do with cards in the book *Games and Fun with Playing Cards* by Joseph Leeming.

29. Painting – Discover the joy of painting on traditional canvas or unusual objects, such as rocks!

30. Create Paper Airplanes and fly them.

31. Learning how to make, throw and catch boomerangs with the book *Boomerangs – How to Make and Throw Them* by Bernard Mason.

32. Archery – Learn the basics of bow and arrow techniques.

33. Participate in a Photographic Scavenger Hunt – take digital photographs of each item required.

34. Create the Ultimate Pandemic Facial Mask complete with embellishments

and accessories and a one-minute infomercial to sell the fine points of your design.

35. Hula Hoop your way to fun and fitness.

36. Cycling - There's plenty of room for physical distancing in this activity and opportunities to learn basic bicycle maintenance and repair.

37. Paddle Boarding – One of the newest solo paddle sports. Great for building strength and balance.

38. Kayaking – a traditional solo paddling activity, with a bit more stability.

39. Frisbee Golf and Foot Golf – Two variations on a theme. Frisbee or Disc Golf is popular and many communities have courses. Just be sure to sanitize the discs between players. Foot Golf is played on a regular golf course, with a soccer ball and 21-inch diameter holes.

40. Geocaching – A seek and find treasure-hunting activity, perfect for summer camps. Learn more at Geocaching.com.

41. Calisthenics – A physical training technique that uses bodyweight instead of additional equipment. Learn more at SchoolOfCalisthenics.com.

42. Gardening – Indoors or out, growing plants, flowers, trees and vegetables is fun.

43. Show Your Gratitude – In the book *59 Seconds,* Richard Wiseman reveals that having people list three things that they are grateful for in their life or to reflect on three events that have gone especially well recently can significantly increase their level of happiness for about a month. This, in turn, can cause them to be more optimistic about the future and can improve their physical health.

44. Practice Calligraphy – And other fancy lettering forms. Learn the basics at ThePostmansKnock.com/beginners-guide-modern-calligraphy/.

45. Watch the Sunrise (or Sunset).

46. Bake – Most people enjoy a home-baked desert. Why not learn how to make one yourself? Pies, cookies, cakes and more await you.

47. Learn to Cook a New Dish – Learn how to make your favorite dish. Mine was turkey pot pie, with my Thanksgiving leftovers. You'll find the online recipe here: AllRecipes.com/recipe/9230/turkey-pot-pie/.

48. Photography – Find a creative way to share photographs, or try to capture the letters A-Z by taking photographs of things around you that look like these letters.

49. Drum Circle – participate in a physically distanced drum circle with your friends.

50. Eat a Late Dinner by Candlelight.

51. Make a List (of all the things you want to do when the pandemic is over).

52. Learn how to whittle or carve wood. Nothing feels as good as carving a good piece of wood into a keepsake that will last forever.

53. Surfing – There are plenty of outdoor sports that lend themselves to physical distancing, and provided you have an ocean nearby, surfing can be one of them.

54. Slingshot Target Shooting – Using kernels of corn or dry dog food pellets as ammunition (to feed birds and other wildlife). Set up a target range with tin and other metal targets (which make a satisfying sound when hit).

55. Virtual Activities Online, including Scavenger Hunts and Escape Rooms.

56. Fishing – Another outdoor activity that lends itself to appropriate physical distancing, especially fly fishing and other casting styles.

57. Outdoor Cooking – Plenty of opportunities here for everything from Dutch Oven cooking to grilling, to pie irons in the fire to Jiffy Pop popcorn.

58. Hiking and Backpacking – Two great ways to explore nature, exercise and spend time in the great outdoors.

59. Walking – A sometimes overlooked activity that lowers anxiety, improves health and increases optimism.

60. Jumping Rope – solo rope jumping is an amazing way to promote cardiovascular health and fitness. There are also some very cool jump rope tricks presented at JumpRopeDudes.com.

61. Build a Sand Castle – A time honored tradition of beach art, using local resources.

62. Making & Flying Kites – two perfectly great ideas for camp.

63. Build a Snowman (in the winter) or Make an Ice Carving (from blocks of ice in the summer).

64. Write a Postcard to a Friend.

65. Mountain Biking – Another great outdoor activity that tends to create appropriate physical distancing.

66. Hopscotch – And other solo sidewalk games.

67. Sample a New Food – Eat something new for the very first time.

68. Invent a Non-Contact Handshake or Greeting.

69. Read an e-book.

70. Make a Snow Angel (or a sand angel, or a mud angel...).

71. Learn to solve a Rubik's Cub

72. Play Tennis – Another outdoor game with appropriate physical distancing.

73. Translate a Word, Phrase or Message into a Foreign Language, using Translate.Google.com.

74. Zumba – Learn how to do this musical fitness activity.

75. Host a Fashion Show – Using the theme of your choice.

76. Have a Trivia Party.

77. Start a Diary.

78. Learn to Draw - Starting with the book *Drawing on the Right Side of the Brain* by Betty Edwards.

79. Create a comic strip or a meme using images from the Internet.

80. Write a Thank You Note.

81. Parkour – Learn this very physical combination of fitness, running, gymnastics and acrobatics from the World Freerunning Parkour Federation at WFPF.com.

101 ADDITIONAL PHYSICALLY DISTANCED ACTIVITIES

82. Create a Flash Mob Dance Presentation.

83. Create a Scrapbook of Memories.

84. Bird Watching – Another wonderful opportunity to be outside and get some fresh air. Learn more at BirdWatchingDaily.com.

85. Piloting a Drone – Fun and Games in wide open spaces.

86. Blogging – Find a subject that interests you and write about it, online. 87. Songwriting – Use your musical talents to compose the lyrics or music to a song. Then perform it for your friends.

87. Create temporary art - on a sidewalk, on the beach, or wherever else you can find

88. Quilting – A time-honored tradition and a great thing to do with all those leftover pieces of fabric.

89. Knitting, Crocheting and Weaving – Another time-honored tradition of handcrafting

90. Carpentry and the Fine Art of Woodworking.

91. Skipping Stones – and other simple pleasures by the waterfront.

92. Yo-Yoing – Learn incredible tricks and stunts practiced by world champions at Yo-Yo.com.

93. Snorkeling – An adventurous water sport (just be sure to sanitize the equipment between participants).

94. Scuba Diving – All the elements of physical distancing, including your

own air supply.

95. Pilates – A low-impact exercise consisting of flexibility, muscular strength and endurance movements. Learn more at Pilates.com.

97. Skateboarding (and Mountainboarding).

98. Learn Magic, Sleight of Hand and Hand Manipulations.

99. Start a Collection – Find something you appreciate (sea shells, buttons, stones, antique silverware) and collect as many as you can, and then display these items for all to appreciate.

100. Extreme Ironing – For those photogenically adventurous this extreme sport invites athletes to transport an ironing board, iron and shirt to remote locations and photograph their talents. Learn more at CoolOfTheWild.com/extreme-ironing/.

101. Build an Inuksuit - Build an Inuksuit or create a tower by stacking rocks on top of each other.

16

Risk Assessment Checklist

A Filter for Group Activities

When assessing any activity for risk at the moment, we have put together the following simple checklist. We hope this makes the job of knowing what we can do (and what we can't) much simpler.

If you can answer Yes to two or more of these questions, then it might be best to temporarily suspend using that particular activity, replace it with another more suitable (and lower risk) activity, or modify the activity to reduce the level of risk.

Does the activity:

1. Place participants in close proximity with each other? Yes No
2. Involve singing, shouting, chanting or cheering? Yes No
3. Create physical contact between players? Yes No
4. Involve a shared resource, touched by many? Yes No

5. Take place indoors? Yes No
6. Take place in a space with poor ventilation? Yes No
7. Require more people than a standard cohort group? Yes No
8. Require equipment that cannot be sanitized between groups? Yes No
9. Require hand-washing before and after the activity? Yes No

17

Best Practices To Minimize Risk

Here is a brief and by no means comprehensive list of best practices and recommendations for real-world in-person events, such as summer camps, schools and colleges, conferences and other group gatherings.

Everything you can do to minimize risk to your participants and staff is a step in the right direction and the more techniques you employ, the lower the risk.

Physical distancing. A minimum of six feet (two meters) between participants at all times.

Use outdoor, well-ventilated spaces whenever possible.

Wear masks or facial coverings (properly) as recommended by health authorities.

Avoid shared resources handled by multiple participants and staff.

Sanitize any community equipment after each use.

Reduce capacity. Decrease the total number of participants occupying a particular space or attending the event. Avoid large group gatherings.

Avoid activities that require physical contact (such as tag games, low element rope course safety spotting, square dancing, etc.), that bring participants into close proximity with each other or that include singing, shouting, chanting or cheering.

Wash hands frequently using soap and water or hand sanitizer.

Daily health checks for Covid-19 symptoms, including temperature measurement.

Organize small groups into cohorts that do not mingle with other cohort groups.

Be prepared to initiate contact tracing if necessary.

Pre-Event Self-Quarantining. Participants and Staff should refrain from other public gatherings prior to the dates of the event (10-14 days or per local health recommendations).

Create a physical distancing reminder that integrates the theme or focus of your event. Just be sure to create a technique that doesn't grow old after a dozen or more uses each day. Preliminary research results from the American Camp Association indicates that during the summer of 2020, both campers and staff found maintaining physical distance one of the most difficult challenges at camp. Chances are, you will have to remind participants often, so find a creative and pleasant way to do so.

And finally, exceed all of these best practices whenever possible!

18

What The Research Tells Us

What the Research Tells Us

One of the most comprehensive research studies conducted in the past year was performed by the American Camp Association (ACACamps.org) and focused primarily on resident and day camps in the United States. You can review the complete findings of the Camp Counts 2020 research study at: www.acacamps.org/resource-library/research/campcounts-2020-report.

Some of the significant findings from this study include:

Approximately 2/3 of the day camps in the United States operated during the summer of 2020, compared to about 1/3 of the resident (overnight) camps. Approximately 90% of camps in the USA are planning to operate in the summer of 2021.

Overnight camps that did not operate, even under modified conditions, attributed their decision to: prohibitions from state or local health departments (58%), serving a population of campers with vulnerable health conditions (19%), inability to secure sufficient PPE and supplies to meet precaution standards (15%) and the inability to maintain camp culture and traditions under the necessary pandemic protocols (60%).

Camps that did operate incorporated a variety of non-pharmaceutical interventions (NPI's), including: increased cleaning practices, sanitizing community resources frequently, periodic checks for Covid-19 symptoms, pre-screening campers and staff prior to arriving at camp, personal protective equipment (such as masks), hand washing, testing, physical distancing, cohorts and minimization of contact between cohort groups, modifications to daily schedule and activities, modifications to meals and dining hall practices, increased outdoor activities, ventilation of indoor spaces, reduced enrollment and increased communication with parents/guardians throughout the camp experience. Of these actions, the wearing of face masks, physical distancing and conducting a majority of camp activities outdoors (in well ventilated areas) were deemed the most significant in the mitigation of Covid-19.

Both campers and camp staff responded that the two most difficult aspects of camp under pandemic protocols were maintaining appropriate physical distancing and the wearing of masks. Parents cited difficulties because of frequent changes in camp policies and procedures as the pandemic continued, and not being allowed onsite during camper drop-off and pick-up. Camps directors mentioned that the most-costly aspects of camp this year included additional cleaning, extra staff required to meet guidelines, PPE and testing of campers and staff.

19

References And Resources

While the most recent information on physical distancing and safely emerging from the effects of the Covid-19 pandemic is available on the internet, there are several helpful resources now in print to help you in your quest to provide in-person real-world programs and to fill these events with activities that meet or exceed current standards related to gatherings of all sizes.

Many of these publications are available from the American Camp Association bookstore (ACABookstore.org), Training-Wheels Inc. (Training-Wheels.com) and Amazon.com.

For health regulations, guidelines for physical distancing and other Covid-19 related best practices, including the *Field Guide for Camps*, visit the Covid-19 Resource Center on the American Camp Association website (www.aca-camps.org).

The Dutchman's Rope – A unique way to maintain physical distancing during real-world in-person gatherings by Jim Cain (ISBN 978-1-6067-9519-4). Twenty-five group activities and best practices that minimize risk. Make your own Dutchman's Rope from these instructions or purchase a hand-crafted rope from Training-Wheels.com (1-888-553-0147) in the United States, Adven-

REFERENCES AND RESOURCES

tureworks.org (1-877-311-5683) in Canada, RSVP Design (RSVPDesign.co.uk) in the United Kingdom, Serious Learning Tool (SeriousLearningTool.com) in Hong Kong and Innotrek / Next Factor (NextFactor.com.sg) in Singapore.

Teambuilding with Index Cards - 180 activities for teachers, trainers, facilitators and group leaders of all kinds that turn ordinary index and playing cards into extraordinary teaching tools by Jim Cain, ISBN 978-1-5249-6498-6. You'll be amazed how much you can do with index cards, after which you can recycle them!

Find Something To Do! by Jim Cain, ISBN 978-0-9882046-0-7. A collection of more than 130 powerful activities with no equipment at all, so there's nothing to sanitize after the game is over!

100 Activities That Build Unity, Community & Connection by Jim Cain, ISBN 978-1-60679-374-9. An outstanding collection of games and activities that build connection. Just what the world needs most right now.

The Revised and Expanded Book of Raccoon Circles by Tom Smith and Jim Cain, ISBN 978-0-7575-3265-8. You'll be amazed how many activities you can facilitate with a single teambuilding prop.

The Learning Curve, ISBN 978-1-6067-9501-9. Navigating the Transition from Facilitating in the Real World to Facilitating in a Virtual One. Random Thoughts, Helpful Insights, Half-Baked Ideas, Suggestions and Other Useful Information from the Virtual Facilitation Practice Group.

101 Games to Play Whilst Socially Distancing by Martin Williams, ISBN 979-8-6490-8830-5. Book 1, for children aged 3-7.

101 More Games to Play Whilst Socially Distancing by Martin Williams, ISBN 979-8-6817-6475-5. Book 2, for children aged 3-7.

Together by Vivek Murthy – 19th Surgeon General of the United States, ISBN 978-0-0629-1329-6. The Healing Power of Human Connection in a Sometimes Lonely World

Bet You Can't Do This! Impossible Tricks to Astound Your Friends by Sandy Ransford, ISBN 978-0-3303-9772-8. Plenty of silly fun, including activities which can easily be adapted for physical distancing.

How to Do Nothing with Nobody All Alone by Yourself by Robert Paul Smith, ISBN 978-0-9820-5395-9. Self-made fun and more.

Everyman's Book of Solo Games by Gyles Brandreth, ISBN 978-0-4600-4564-4. Over 300 solo games that can be played simultaneously with others nearby.

Extraordinary Facilitation by Jim Cain, ISBN 978-1-6067-9507-1. Insights from half a century of working and playing with groups. A lifetime of facilitation advice.

20

About The Authors

Martin Williams

Martin Williams is the founder of the training company Early Impact. He has worked in early education in the UK for ten years, teaching children between the ages of 3 and 5. He is driven by a determination to make early learning exciting and engaging for both children and adults.

In his work with Early Impact, he has trained thousands of teachers and

ABOUT THE AUTHORS

practitioners in many of the key areas of education. He has delivered school improvement projects for authorities, and he has led training for local early years quality teams.

He blogs and writes about all the educational topics he believes he can make a difference in, and he is strongly committed to sharing information and helping others as much as he can. You can find his blog by going to earlyimpactlearning.com

He is passionate about the 'practical' nature of learning both for adults and children. All of his courses are fast-paced, interactive, and contain a multitude of real-life resources that attendees try out.

He runs hands-on training courses in face-to-face venues across the North of England and the Midlands, specialising in early phonics, mathematics, fine motor and mark-making.

He delivers popular online training sessions through Early Impact's website which you can find here - earlyimpactlearning.com/online-courses/

Jim Cain and Teamwork & Teamplay

Dr. Jim Cain is the author of twenty-three texts filled with powerful team and community building activities from around the world. His train-the-trainer workshops are legendary in the adventure-based learning world and have taken him to all fifty states and thirty-six countries (so far). He is the innovator of over forty teambuilding activities used by corporations, colleges, camps, conferences and communities. Jim likes to share his unique collection of team challenges, games, puzzles and training techniques with audiences of all kinds, all over the world.

Jim is also the creative mind behind the active-learning company Teamwork & Teamplay, which provides staff trainings, teambuilding equipment, debriefing tools, curriculum development, reference books, conference workshops, keynote (playnote) presentations and teambuilding consulting services around the world. Virtually and in-person too.

For more information about the contents of this book, physical distancing and teambuilding in general, contact Jim Cain using the information shown here.

Jim Cain, Ph.D.
Teamwork & Teamplay

468 Salmon Creek Road
Brockport, New York 14420 USA

Phone +1 (585) 637-0328

jimcain@teamworkandteamplay.com
www.teamworkandteamplay.com

Also by Martin Williams and Dr. Jim Cain

Other books include...

101 Games To Play Whilst Socially Distancing, by Martin Williams

The Amazon #1 Bestseller.

Attempting social distancing with young children raises many questions.

Split into 12 areas of the curriculum, this book offers 101 scintillating games to play in the context of social distancing for children aged 3-7.

I have been on several of Martin's courses...and been blown away by all the ideas and suggestions he has for Early Years. This book is no different!! Superb!
   Rosie, Review on Amazon

I am so excited about this book!! This book is a GODSEND. It is so well written and well structured, so easy to read... I wholeheartedly endorse it. Such a handy resource!!
   Sunshan, Review on Amazon

101 More Games To Play Whilst Socially Distancing, by Martin Williams

The bestselling sequel.

101 more imaginative games to help children stay happy, healthy and learning in the 'new normal.'

This book is an amazing sequel to 101 games to play whilst social distancing. I have been trying out different games with the children I teach (Nursery-Yr1). There are some lovely games for promoting well-being and discussing emotions with children which has been invaluable in this uncertain climate. A great book and an amazing resource for any classroom.
   Candice, Review on Amazon

Once again, another well thought out, imaginative set of games to add to the armoury. This book, along with its predecessor has a myriad of engaging and inspirational games which hold the attention of the players with no difficulty at all – a winner on all counts when my job is made easier! Highly recommended for all types of educator and parents too!
   Mrs C M C Ashby, Review on Amazon

Squiggle, Fiddle, Splat - 101 Genius Fine Motor And Early Writing Activities, by Martin Williams

Early education teachers have a major problem on their hands – many children just aren't interested in anything to do with fine motor or early writing any more.

The number of children with fine motor difficulties is increasing year on year. Teaching early writing becomes harder and harder with every passing day. So, what can we do?

Read this book to find out all the answers, and particularly to learn how to provide games that are scintillating...inspiring...alluring...that are strongly tapped into the interests of the children, and are something they cannot resist!

Review

What a fabulously practical resource!

If, like me, you have accumulated a pile of 'teaching books' that you never get around to reading- buy this and put it straight to the top of your list. READ IT STRAIGHTAWAY!

Helen Dillon, Review on Amazon

Loose Parts Play - A Beginner's Guide, by Martin Williams and Debby Stevens

Looking to unleash the powerful learning potential of loose parts play, but don't know how to begin...

Loose parts play offers a magical and wonder-filled way to deliver learning across the whole curriculum. But there are many things you need to know to get started on the correct footing (and many things that will go wrong if you don't)...

Bursting with more than 200 practical ideas, activities and provocations, this is the perfect guidebook for anyone looking to develop an outstanding loose parts curriculum either at work or at home.

I particularly like that this is a child-led approach and that the resources are simple everyday objects. It is great to see the imagination and creativity it encourages in our pupils - this is the reason why most of us entered the profession. This is a brilliant book and I will be digesting its ideas for some time.
   Gregg, Review on Amazon

Excellent insight into loose parts play. Accessible for both teachers and parents, lots of inspiring ideas and examples. Wish I had read this for my children! Would highly recommend.
   Nicky L, Review on Amazon

The Dutchman's Rope, by Dr. Jim Cain

The Dutchman's Rope - a unique way to maintain physical distancing during real-world in-person gatherings and events by turning a 17th century maritime navigation technique into a 21st century physical distancing tool.

This publication includes best practices and over two dozen activities with appropriate physical distancing.

Anytime a group of people gather together there is an atavistic human instinct to draw closer. Closer to the speaker so to be able to hear what is being said. Closer to friends and family. Close enough to shake hands (if you still remember doing such things). Close enough to hug.

Hopefully we'll be able to return to such things in the near future, but for the next year or so, maintaining physical distance and wearing appropriate face coverings is going to be the norm for many summer camps, conferences and group gatherings.

The most innovative and versatile teambuilding rope since the Raccoon Circle.
   Dr. Jim Cain

Connection Without Contact, by Dr. Jim Cain

Connection Without Contact answers the vital question posed by camp professionals, teachers, trainers, facilitators and group leaders of all kinds...."so, what can we do?"

Pulling data from the American Camp Association's CampCounts 2020 research study and supplementing it with interviews from camp directors, youth development specialists and medical professionals, this book shares cutting-edge best practices for real-world in-person gatherings in a pandemic world.

It also features fifty world-class activities, appropriately physically distanced, to help you build unity, community and connection with your next audience.

"Six feet apart but close at heart."
   Ian Roberts - Executive Director, Camp Ho Mita Koda

"In order to recover, we must reconnect."
   Dr. Jim Cain

Available now from ACABookstore.org, Training-Wheels.com and Amazon.com.

Manufactured by Amazon.ca
Bolton, ON